From Little Acorns

101 Modern Haiku to Discover at Home and in the Classroom

Haiku to Enjoy with Children
and Your Inner Child

"Mighty oaks from little acorns grow."

English proverb

From Little Acorns

101 Modern Haiku to Discover at Home and in the Classroom

Haiku to Enjoy with Children
and Your Inner Child

Anna Eklund-Cheong

ISBN (Paperback): 978-1-968966-56-0
ISBN (Hardcover): 978-1-969368-79-0
ISBN (eBook): 978-1-969368-80-6

For Dan, Eric, and Andrew

WITH MANY THANKS

My gratitude goes out to the haiku journal editors who selected my haiku for inclusion in their delightful issues over the past decade. Every acceptance inspired me to keep writing; every nonacceptance challenged me to do better next time. I have learned what constitutes a good haiku from reading your fine journals—thank you! And I offer my sincere appreciation to two seasoned haiku poets and authors, Abigail Friedman and Scott Wiggerman, for their generous feedback on early versions of my manuscript. I also want to give *un petit* shout-out to my Paris writing group, whose members welcomed me into their circle and provided valuable feedback on all my writing—*merci beaucoup, mes amis!* And, most lovingly, thank you to Dan, my best friend and life partner since 1979, for constant support and...nudging.

Contents

Introduction 1

Suggestions for Reading, Enjoying,

    and Discussing Haiku 5

Chapter 1: Winter Melts into Spring 7

Chapter 2: Spring Blossoms into Summer 23

Chapter 3: Summer Ripens into Autumn 35

Chapter 4: Autumn Curls into Winter 49

Chapter 5: All-Season Haiku (or *Senryu*) 61

Publication Credits for Previously Published Poems 69

Appendix: Notes on Learning and Teaching Haiku 76

Glossary 80

Bibliography (References and Sources) 84

    For Adults, Teachers, and Older Students 84

    For Younger Children 86

Further Exploration 87

    Journals, Organizations, Websites, and Presses

Why This Book Came to Be 92

About the Author 93

Introduction

I learned about haiku in seventh grade in the early 1970s. My English teacher said haiku originated in ancient Japan. She said they were nonrhyming three-line poems about nature and had only 17 syllables, arranged in a 5-7-5 syllable structure over their three lines. "Even children can write them," she said. That was it. Easy, right? You likely learned about haiku this way in school, too. (Note: *Haiku* is used for both singular and plural. This is true for all Japanese nouns used in this book.)

In class, we read a few pages of poems by Japanese haiku masters (e.g., Basho, Issa, Buson, and Shiki). There were haiku about frogs and cherry blossoms, crickets and mountains, snow and crows. Then we kids wrote some. We illustrated them, hung a few on the classroom walls, and gathered others into yarn-stitched booklets. The following week, we moved on to longer forms of poetry. But a spark had been kindled in a few of our young hearts for these wondrous, surprising tiny poems. They seemed so simple at first glance, but they resonated with us. You may even remember, as I do, feeling those little "Aha!" moments when reading the masters' haiku—when the light bulbs above our comic-book selves lit up. And you may have wondered, as I did: Could I write haiku like these someday?

A voracious reader of sci-fi and fantasy novels, I loved poetry, too. I worked in libraries during high school and university and later wrote and edited marketing materials for a publishing company. As a parent, I loved reading poetry to my children. I volunteered every year to help with the poetry units that their teachers prepared.

I encouraged the students I tutored to use more specific nouns and more interesting verbs in their poems: perhaps *chickadee* or *cardinal* instead of *bird*, for example, or *dashed* or *sprinted* instead of *ran*. I urged them to use more of their senses when evoking a scene, describing what is seen, yes, but also what is heard, smelled, touched, or tasted. Together we explored poetic devices such as alliteration, consonance, and assonance; metaphor, simile, and allusion; rhyme and meter; onomatopoeia; personification; and more. This rekindled my interest in haiku, and I started scribbling a few, now and then, in the margins of notebooks.

After my young adult children left home, I dabbled in haiku as a creative outlet. One day, a search on the Internet revealed journals that published haiku. Do I dare? Should I try? I did. I submitted a few haiku to one of the journals, and...nothing. I submitted more haiku to different journals, and all replies were nonacceptances (I have learned not to call them rejections). What was I not getting? What was I doing wrong? It was discouraging. But I was also curious and determined to figure out how to get at least one haiku published in one of those journals. So I subscribed to a few and...What?! These are haiku? Not according to my seventh-grade teacher, they weren't. Some things have changed. Notions about writing haiku in languages other than Japanese have evolved over the last 50 to 60 years. I would have to unlearn a few old things and learn some new ones. And I did. (See "Appendix: Notes on Learning and Teaching Haiku.")

Soon I discovered there was a global haiku community. There are local, regional, national, and international haiku groups worldwide. This community has organized itself into societies. It publishes journals and anthologies; hosts conferences, workshops, and readings; sponsors contests; establishes foundations; and keeps archives of haiku. Members of the global haiku community write scholarly essays on haiku, teach haiku at the university level, mentor other poets, and develop haiku trails through parks and gardens. They have launched websites and podcasts and started haiku pages on social media platforms. I dove right in with an open mind.

I finally had my first haiku accepted for publication in 2015. I was thrilled. Encouraged (and not wanting to be a one-trick pony), I sent out more haiku. Today I have over 130 haiku published in 19 journals and several anthologies. Another dozen haiku have been displayed in the flower boxes of Washington, DC, as part of an annual haiku contest. One of my chapbook manuscripts received an honorable mention in a competition. This journey of discovery, coupled with publishing success, has given me the confidence to teach haiku to others, both children and adults, and to offer my first curated collection in the following pages.

A member of my Paris-based writing group (which includes journalists, authors, teachers, a playwright, a songwriter, and an artist) says this is her favorite haiku in the collection:

one mug of tea . . .
the time it takes frost
to become dew

I wonder which one will be *your* favorite?

Suggestions for Reading, Enjoying, and Discussing Haiku

Read haiku slowly. After each line, pause long enough to let the images and details expand in your mind. Then ask yourself: What is happening in this haiku? Where and when is the action taking place? What does the poet see, hear, smell, taste, or touch? And how does this haiku make me feel? Using your intuition and imagination, think about what larger story might be implied or suggested by the haiku. There can be more than one answer. If the haiku is set in a specific season, does the season play a role in the story? How? (Note: A haiku not set in a seasonal context is sometimes called a *senryu*. Read more about *senryu* in the Glossary.)

It is said that a haiku is only started by the poet, and then it's completed in the reader's mind. Think of a haiku as a quick sketch of a scene or event in which some details are left out. A moment has been captured, but something has been left unsaid. Can you complete the sketch in your mind and imagine some of the details left out? Did you notice that many haiku seemed divided into two parts (often a phrase followed by a fragment, or a fragment followed by a phrase)? Did one part seem to set the haiku's overall scene? Did the other part draw your attention to a detail in that larger scene? Did the haiku present something ordinary in an unusual way? Did the haiku surprise you, make you smile, or feel sad? And, by the end of the haiku, when you discovered the connection between the two parts, did you say to yourself, "Oh, I get it!" Or, perhaps, "Aha!"?

It's time to read some haiku and find out.

Note: Learn more about the fascinating characteristics of modern haiku in the Appendix: Notes on Learning and Teaching Haiku. The basic elements of traditional Japanese haiku are respected, but some changes in structure are needed to account for the many languages that haiku are written in today.

CHAPTER ONE

Winter Melts
into
Spring

first crocus...
last Christmas napkin
under my cup of tea

not yet, daffodils!
tricked by apricity
we're both unprepared

mimosas blooming...
we almost choose a table
on the terrace

forsythia...
the color
of birdsong

if trees
could sing...
magnolia blossoms

oh, magnolia!
if only you'd waited
'til after the storm

spring gusts...
a swirl of dead leaves
in the dugout

spring thaw...
everyone at the dog park
shedding coats

neon reflections
on rainy night streets
...she tugs at her leash

after the downpour
the dog's nose to the ground
mine to the sky

ducks and plum blossoms
arriving together
March wind and sun

mid-March sun...
the playground littered
with little parkas

vernal equinox...
the on-again, off-again
of raincoats

tidal basin stroll...
no buzz, yet
about the first blooms

peak bloom...
the tidal basin rimmed
with tripods

straw baskets in hand...
choosing our *hanami* spot
under pale pink clouds

Hanami means "cherry blossom viewing" in Japanese. The Tidal Basin in Washington, DC, pictured, is renowned for its cherry trees, a gift from Japan given to the city in 1912.

riverside trail...
still leafless enough to see
all the new nests

spring quickening...
chirpier by the day
the birds and I

first warmish day...
an almost finished nest
among swelling buds

spring clover...
all the way back
to skinned knees

rush hour rainbow...
every darting umbrella
tilts up

double rainbow...
fresh handprints appear
low on the window

homemade kites...
the sound of Dad's voice
in warm spring wind

lily-of-the-valley...
Mom's silhouette
at the kitchen sink

just to admire
cascades of wisteria
...May Day stroll

here, there, everywhere!
the randomness
of red poppies

CHAPTER TWO

Spring Blossoms
into
Summer

purple irises…
a hint of hose
in the first sip

water's edge…
I catch myself
falling for lilies

although hidden
behind this hedge
…jasmine

overtaking the garden wall
and all of my senses…
star jasmine

June bugs
rising from the hedge
a Strawberry Moon

one for us
one for the bears...
wild berries

homemade jams...
Grandma always has enough
wooden spoons

drawn to the shoreline
by bright moonlight
... the tide and I

outgoing tide...
the tug of little hands
pulls us to the sea

tide pools
filling and emptying
their pails

sea becoming cloud becoming sea

This is the only *monoku* poem in the collection. Read more about *monoku* in the Glossary.

hydrangeas
wilting in the heat
I water me first

breezeless summer eve...
the bats come out as we
swat! slap! smack! go in

too hot to sleep...
the neighbor's cat and I
startle each other

summer night rain...
conversations seeping deeper
into the porch

cutting garden...
the bees and I both leave with
lavender-scented hands

midsummer harvest...
wildflower seeds
yield butterflies

learning to count
a baker's dozen...
sweetcorn stand

stones, shells, and sea glass...
bits of summer tumbling
from sandy pockets

summer's end...
all the days at the beach
stuffed into this tote

end of summer...
a whiff of campfire smoke
from the laundry heap

CHAPTER THREE

Summer Ripens
into
Autumn

scent of apples...
I hang again upside down
from monkey bars

apple orchard
red, crisp, and crunchy
leaves underfoot

sharing our bounty...
leaving a few apples
on the trees

warm apple crumble...
a last swoop of swallows
foreshadows bats... and stars

first day of school…
faces a little longer
old jeans too short

autumn equilux…
late patio tomatoes
half red, half green

fall festival...
the bees, too, know how few
days of warmth remain

hydrangeas
morphing from rose to plum
an autumn dusk

garden gleaning...
the last of the lavender
we leave for the bees

the last bees
in the last blossoms...
a bud vase will suffice

the first and last flowers
to grace the garden...
seeds I did not sow

pumpkins and mums...
how farmers' markets mark
the passage of time

a heron's stillness
across a birch-gold river
... and my own

taking the longer route...
although they're grown by now
the vixen's kits

rustle and crunch...
eyes closed, listening
to October sun

October *plein-air*...
two painters share fresh tubes of
cyan and orange

illuminating our hunt
for the winter quilts...
October's full moon

finally finding
behind the Easter baskets
the jack-o-lanterns

autumn plantings...
the squirrels and I choose
the same spots

November nightfall...
a wren and a mouse
also hurry home

missing the bats
but not the mosquitoes...
ah! Beaver Moon

rain again . . .
I set soup beans
out to soak

first frost . . .
last cherry tomatoes
catching rays on the sill

CHAPTER FOUR

Autumn Curls
into
Winter

first rays of sun
on morning frost...
I'll catch the next train

just one more cup...
the sparkle of morning sun
on frosted pines

one mug of tea...
the time it takes frost
to become dew

the air tinged
with the promise of snow
filling the bird feeders

first snowfall…
the hard-boiled eggs
overcooked

a hush falls over
the office chatter...
first flurries

a flurry of coats
flies from the closets...
first downy flakes

sticking to dark bark
the first snowfall glistening...
digging for mittens

last sled on the slope
rosy cheeks and frozen toes...
they'll sleep well tonight

snowdrifts...
mounds of sodden mittens
melting on the rug

winter rain...
outdoor café tables drip
as we sip from inside

gray December day...
the woodpecker's red crown
almost glows

puzzle weather...
we rise only to forage
for cinnamon sticks

taking out the trash...
a fingernail moon
just beyond Orion's grasp

each gust tugs
at their ragged gowns
… winter willows

neglected garden …
dry hydrangea heads
bent in heavy snow

New Year's Day dawning...
city streets full of quiet
and noisy birdsong

mid-winter snow
piling up in the mailbox
seed catalogs

rainy day...
the egg on my galette
sunny side up

CHAPTER FIVE

All-Season
Haiku
(sometimes called *senryu*)

sliver of moon
sinking slowly out of view...
the fever breaks near dawn

crack of dawn...
Crayola's biggest box
not up to the task

all the world's problems
solved before dessert
… kitchen table

my aunts' voices
percolating in the kitchen
Mom's old coffee pot

yard sale...
Eeyore and Chewbacca
having tea

dusty stuffed dragon...
the spells cast long ago
from cardboard castles

a fledgling teeters
on the edge of a nest
…I pack his socks

arrivals gate
all faces the same
until yours

a lump in my throat
I knot the bow tie at his
… and let go

downsizing…
still unable to pitch
their pinch pots

from little acorns...
our grandson now plays with
his father's old toys

One last haiku for my guys...
Love, Mom

raining cats and dogs...
sprawled on the floor, giggling
a "puddle of monkeys"

Publication Credits for Previously Published Poems

SPRING POEMS

first crocus . . .
The Heron's Nest, Vol. XVII, No. 4, Dec. 2015

not yet, daffodils! . . .
Autumn Moon Haiku Journal, 7:2, Spring/Summer 2024

forsythia . . .
Cattails, April 2021

if trees . . .
Cold Moon Journal, Dec. 2022

oh, magnolia! . . .
Blithe Spirit, 34.2, May 2024

spring gusts . . .
Tinywords, 20.1, May 4, 2020

spring thaw . . .
Golden Haiku Contest, 2019, *Judges' Favorites*

neon reflections . . .
BHS Members' Anthology 2020

after the downpour . . .
Blithe Spirit, 31.1, Feb. 2021

mid-March sun . . .
Golden Haiku Contest, 2018, *Honorable Mention*

vernal equinox . . .
Blithe Spirit, 35.2, May 2025

tidal basin stroll . . .
Golden Haiku Contest, 2024

peak bloom . . .
Golden Haiku Contest, 2019, *Judges' Favorites*

straw baskets in hand . . .
Nick Virgilio Haiku Assoc. *"Haiku in Action,"* April 8, 2021

riverside trail . . .
Autumn Moon Haiku Journal, 6:2, Spring/Summer 2023

spring clover . . .
Visiting the Wind: HSA Members' Anthology 2021

rush-hour rainbow . . .
Dawn Returns: HSA Members' Anthology 2022

double rainbow . . .
Under the Basho, Nov. 2024

homemade kites . . .
Blithe Spirit, 31.4, Nov. 2021

lily-of-the-valley . . .
Blithe Spirit, 30.3, Aug. 2020

here, there, everywhere . . .
Presence, No. 79, July 2024

SUMMER POEMS

purple irises . . .
The Heron's Nest, Vol. XXII, No. 3, Sept. 2020

water's edge . . .
Ekphrasis—BHS Members' Anthology 2017

although hidden . . .
Blithe Spirit, 30.1, Feb. 2020

overtaking the garden wall . . .
Blithe Spirit, 33.2, May 2023

June bugs . . .
Blithe Spirit, 30.3, Aug. 2020

one for us . . .
Presence, No. 75, March 2023

homemade jams . . .
Cold Moon Journal, May 2025

drawn to the shoreline . . .
Presence, No. 72, March 2022

outgoing tide . . .
Tinywords, 23.1, May 16, 2023

tide pools . . .
Earthworks: HNA Conference Anthology 2023

sea becoming cloud . . .
BHS Members' Anthology 2022

hydrangeas . . .
Blithe Spirit, 27.4, Nov. 2017

too hot to sleep . . .
Hedgerow, No. 131, 2020

summer night rain . . .
Blithe Spirit, 34.3, Aug. 2024

cutting garden . . .
Under the Basho, Nov. 2024

midsummer harvest . . .
On Down the Road: HSA Members' Anthology 2017

learning to count . . .
The Heron's Nest, Vol. XXVII, No. 1, March 2025

summer's end . . .
The Heron's Nest, Vol. XIX, No. 3, Sept. 2017

end of summer . . .
Blithe Spirit, 27.4, Nov. 2017

AUTUMN POEMS

scent of apples . . .
Blithe Spirit, 30.1, Feb. 2020

apple orchard . . .
Blithe Spirit, 27.4, Nov. 2017

sharing our bounty . . .
Frogpond, 44.1, Winter 2021

warm apple crumble . . .
Blithe Spirit, 30.3, Aug. 2020

first day of school . . .
Cattails, April 2021

autumn equilux . . .
Blithe Spirit, 32.4, Nov. 2022

fall festival . . .
BHS Members' Anthology 2023

hydrangeas . . .
Scarlet Dragonfly Journal, Nov. 10, 2022

garden gleaning . . .
Blithe Spirit, 34.4, Nov. 2024

the last bees . . .
Hauling the Tide: HSA Members' Anthology 2024

the first and last flowers . . .
Wales Haiku Journal, Spring 2021

a heron's stillness . . .
Presence, No. 68, Nov. 2020

taking the longer route . . .
Presence, No. 76, July 2023

rustle and crunch . . .
Blithe Spirit, 31.1, Feb. 2021

October plein-air . . .
Blithe Spirit, 31.4, Nov. 2021

illuminating our hunt . . .
Tsuri-Doro, No. 25, Jan./Feb. 2025

autumn plantings . . .
Golden Haiku Contest, 2017

November nightfall . . .
Blithe Spirit, 29.2, May 2019

rain again . . .
Frogpond, 43.2, Spring/Summer 2020

first frost . . .
Autumn Moon Haiku Journal, 6:1,
Autumn/Winter 2022/23

WINTER POEMS

first rays of sun . . .
Tinywords, 21.1, April 12, 2021

just one more cup . . .
Under the Basho, October 2022

one mug of tea . . .
Presence, No. 70, July 2021

the air tinged . . .
Blithe Spirit, 31.1, Feb. 2021

first snowfall . . .
Blithe Spirit, 30.2, May 2020

a hush falls over . . .
Presence, No. 75, March 2023

sticking to dark bark . . .
Golden Haiku Contest, 2015/16

last sled on the slope . . .
Golden Haiku Contest, 2015/16

snowdrifts . . .
Blithe Spirit, 28.1, Feb. 2018

gray December day . . .
Presence, No. 69, March 2021

puzzle weather . . .
Autumn Moon Haiku Journal, 8:1,
Autumn/Winter 2024/25

taking out the trash . . .
Blithe Spirit, 29.2, May 2019

each gust tugs . . .
Presence, No. 69, March 2021

neglected garden . . .
Cold Moon Journal, May 2025

mid-winter snow . . .
Blithe Spirit, 31.2, May 2021

rainy day . . .
Failed Haiku, Vol. 6, No. 64, 2021

sliver of moon . . .
Presence, No. 80, Nov. 2024

crack of dawn . . .
Failed Haiku, Vol. 5, No. 53, 2020

all the world's problems . . .
BHS Members' Anthology 2021

my aunts' voices . . .
Mayfly, Issue 72, 2022

yard sale . . .
Failed Haiku, Vol. 5, No. 53, 2020

stuffed dragon . . .
Fired Up Haiku, Bicadeideias, Portugal, 2024

a fledgling teeters . . .
Bundled Wildflowers: HSA Members' Anthology 2020

arrivals gate . . .
Acorn, No. 35, Fall 2015

a lump in my throat . . .
Modern Haiku, 54.1, Winter/Spring 2023

downsizing . . .
Frogpond, Vol. 44.2, Spring/Summer 2021

Minor punctuation and word changes were made to a few haiku since their first publication in various journals and anthologies.

Appendix
Notes on Learning and Teaching Haiku

In ancient Japan, a guest at a *renga* gathering (a meeting of friends or scholars organized for the writing of linked collaborative poems called *renga*) would be asked to open the poetry-writing session with a *hokku* (an opening verse) written for the occasion. Participants then took turns adding their verses to the collectively composed poem. A good *hokku* would get the poetry-writing party off to a good start. The *hokku* referenced a season and usually acknowledged the host or setting of the party in some way. *Hokku* writers were respected for their poetic prowess. Eventually, in the 17th century, the best *hokku*, from noted masters such as Basho, were appreciated enough to be collected and published as stand-alone poems. They were prized for their evocativeness, simple language, connection to nature, and occasional allusions to well-known classic poems.

Hokku were traditionally composed of 17 language sounds called *on* (pronounced "own"; similar to syllables in English, but typically shorter, among other differences). Written vertically down a page in a single line in Japanese characters, the phrasing of the verse usually broke into groups of 5, 7, and 5 sound units, although other sound patterns can be found, too. Included in the 5-7-5 sound count were *kireji* (sounds or words that act as spoken punctuation).

Toward the end of the 19th century, the Japanese poet Masaoka Shiki proposed that stand-alone *hokku* (those not intended to start a *renga*) should be called *haiku*, meaning "light verse." The word *haiku* has been used worldwide since Shiki's time.

When I teach haiku workshops for adults, I ask participants to reconsider the 5-7-5 syllable notion of haiku they may have held for many years. The challenge of writing something meaningful in a 5-7-5 syllable pattern is fun, certainly, but it is not the only way to write haiku—and *not* the most important thing. Haiku is poetry, after all, not a syllable-counting exercise. Many serious haiku poets began with the 5-7-5 form and then learned to write a more modern-style haiku, with a looser structure, as they read more about the differences between the English and Japanese languages. Japanese-language haiku written in phrases of 5-7-5 *on* typically have fewer words than English-language haiku written with 17 syllables (which could have as many as 17 words). Most modern literary haiku published today, in English and other non-Japanese languages, are shorter than 17 syllables to more closely approximate the content of Japanese haiku.

Michael Dylan Welch, a poet regarded as an authority in the haiku community, has a couple of essays on this topic on his websites: nahaiwrimo.com/why-no-5-7-5 and graceguts.com/essays/the-discipline-of-haiku.

Haiku poets also experiment with writing in one to four lines, although writing in three remains the most common format. Even the tradition of including a season word is less important for many modern haiku poets. (Note: Haiku-like poems without seasonal references, and featuring human behavior in human-made settings, may be called *senryu* by some.) Several haiku community commentators have suggested that a new genre of short-form poetry has evolved from traditional Japanese haiku—called modern English-Language Haiku (ELH).

If three lines in a 5-7-5 syllable pattern are not necessary for a poem to be called a haiku, what then *is* required? What is more critical for haiku than a prescribed form? What do haiku journal editors look for when deciding whether or not a haiku is well written?

Experienced haiku poets generally agree that the following haiku characteristics are more important than strict syllable counts:

1) Haiku are short, usually about one breath long, using up to (but often far fewer than) 17 syllables. Say just enough, but no more.

2) Haiku phrasing flows naturally, uses plain language, proper grammar, and good syntax. A fragment/phrase or phrase/fragment structure is common.

3) Haiku typically contain two juxtaposed images with a slight disjunction between them. There is usually a break, called *kire* in Japanese, between the two images. Readers complete the haiku in their minds through intuition and imagination.

4) Haiku capture a single moment and are written in the present tense. This heightens the feeling of immediacy.

5) Haiku use objective descriptions of scenes or events that have been experienced through one or more of the poet's five senses. Avoid opinions and abstract words.

6) Haiku traditionally include season words or references, called *kigo* in Japanese, or they connect the human-made world to the natural world.

7) Haiku should "show," but not "tell," the emotion the poet is feeling. Sketch a scene that evokes in your readers the same emotion you felt when you were inspired to write your haiku; do not tell them how you felt. Allow the imagery to work without interpretation.

8) Haiku often suggest or imply a larger story that readers must infer for themselves.

9) Haiku poets avoid rhyme, overt metaphor, and simile. Haiku have no titles. They use minimal punctuation, and often none. Haiku poets do not capitalize the first word of each line, do not end haiku with periods, and avoid writing haiku that read as sentences.

10) The best haiku evoke an experience of connection or insight, revelation, or even epiphany. This is called the "Aha!" moment in haiku. Effective haiku resonate with readers.

Most haiku journal editors will accept a 5-7-5 haiku if it also embodies the features listed above. Of course, readers will find exceptions to this normative ideal. Many editors allow for some skilled artistic or poetic license. The Haiku Foundation presents common conventions of modern haiku here: thehaikufoundation.org/contemporary-haiku.

Haiku are not three-line lists of items, nor are they three-line descriptions of a single thing. There must be a space for readers to enter the haiku, engage with the images, and discover the suggested meaning and emotion for themselves. Effective haiku often contain juxtaposed scenes or events that hint at a contrast or a comparison. Haiku are fully realized only when readers use their imagination and intuition to discover the implied stories and feelings.

I encourage educators and future haiku poets to dig deeper into the evolution of our understanding of modern English-Language Haiku (ELH). The resources in the Bibliography are excellent places to learn more.

Glossary

A Few Japanese Terms Used in Books About Haiku

Ginko: A walk, typically outdoors in a park or garden or along a trail or beach, taken with the intent to be inspired to write haiku.

Haibun: A Japanese literary art form that presents a short piece of prose, often a vignette, interspersed with one or more haiku. The haiku usually heightens the effect of the prose or deepens its meaning; the prose inspires the haiku, but is not necessarily related to it directly.

Haiga: A Japanese art form that links a haiku to a bit of artwork and presents the two together; the artwork often enhances the haiku's effect, but does not necessarily illustrate the haiku directly.

Haijin: The Japanese word for a haiku poet. When I finish a haiku workshop at a school, I often tell students that after they have written their first haiku, I can call them *haijin*.

Haiku: The Haiku Society of America defines haiku as "a short poem that uses imagistic language to convey the essence of an experience of nature or the season intuitively linked to the human condition." (See <u>hsa-haiku.org/hsa-definitions.html</u>.) Another definition, taken from Jim Kacian's *How to Haiku*: A haiku is "a brief poem which records an experience of a moment of revelation into the nature of the world in an effort to share it with others." (See the full citation in the Bibliography.)

Hokku: The opening stanza of a linked collaboratively written poem called a *renga* or *renku*; it was typically written in 17 *on* (Japanese-language sound units) and included a *kigo* (season word) and a *kireji* (cutting word). After *hokku* became appreciated as stand-alone poems, they were eventually renamed *haiku*.

Kigo: Traditionally, the word or phrase in a haiku that indicates what season the poem is set in; for haiku purposes, there were five main seasons: spring, summer, fall, winter, and the New Year. Not all haiku have *kigo*; sometimes haiku without season words are called *senryu*.

Kire and Kireji: To indicate where the cut (*kire*) is made between the two juxtaposed parts of a haiku, poets writing in Japanese may use a cutting word (*kireji*); these cutting words are vocalized and act almost as spoken punctuation. Some examples of *kireji* are: *ya*, *kana*, *ka*, and *-keri*. Poets writing in English often use punctuation marks, such as an em dash or an ellipsis, to show the cut between the juxtaposed parts in their haiku; the cut between parts can also be implied syntactically.

Kukai: A gathering of haiku writers to share their haiku and (usually anonymously) select their favorites. The haiku brought to the *kukai* are discussed, and the writers learn to improve their haiku through listening and offering feedback.

Monoku: A word coined in 2011 by haiku poet and publisher Jim Kacian, describing haiku written in one horizontal line. The term *monostich* is also used for one-line haiku by some editors.

On: Pronounced "own," the phonetic sound units counted in the Japanese language by its speakers. Some authoritative voices in the haiku community feel that a historical misunderstanding led to the word *on* being incorrectly translated as "syllable" in English. *On* are always short sounds, e.g., *sa-ku-ra*. Many English syllables are longer, sometimes having consonant blends both before and after a vowel sound, for example, *thwart, plunge, splurge, crunch, scourge, clutch, prowl, scratch.*

Renga/Renku: Long, linked collaborative poems written by groups of friends or scholars as a pleasant pastime. After someone in a group offers an opening verse, called a *hokku*, to start a poem, poets add their verses in turns, usually linking to the previous verse and then slightly shifting away from it. Eventually, *hokku* became the haiku we know today.

Saijiki: A book that organizes hundreds of words into seasonal categories to help haiku writers find the perfect *kigo* (season word) for their haiku, which are traditionally set in a seasonal context, often using references to nature and the natural world.

Senryu: From the Haiku Society of America's website: "A *senryu* is a poem, structurally similar to haiku, that highlights the foibles of human nature, usually in a humorous or satiric way." (See more information here: hsa-haiku.org/hsa-definitions.html.) Some haiku community commentators and journal editors also refer to haiku-like poems as *senryu* when they lack a reference to a season or do not connect the natural world to the human-made world; others make no distinction. Many haiku published today might be labeled *senryu* by those who make the distinction. *Senryu* are fun to write and are widely published. These two journals are devoted to the form: *Prune Juice* (prunejuicesenryu.com) and *Failed Haiku* (failedhaiku.com).

Tanka: A classic form of Japanese poetry rendered in five lines in English and traditionally written with 31 Japanese-language sound units called *on*, structured with 5-7-5-7-7 of these units across the five lines. (See the Tanka Society of America for more information: tankasocietyofamerica.org.) Many modern *tanka* are also written in a freer structure in non-Japanese languages.

Bibliography
References, Sources, Recommended Reading
for Adults, Teachers, and Older Students

Burns, Allan, editor, *Where the River Goes: The Nature Tradition in English-Language Haiku* (Ormskirk, UK, Snapshot Press, 2013)

Digregorio, Charlotte, *Haiku and Senryu: A Simple Guide for All* (Winnetka, IL, Artful Communicators Press, 2014)

Donegan, Patricia, *Write Your Own Haiku* (Rutland, VT, Tuttle, 2005, 2017) (Great for school libraries.)

Gurga, Lee, author, and Trumbull, Charles, editor, *Haiku: A Poet's Guide* (Lincoln, IL, Modern Haiku Press, 2003)

Hass, Robert, editor/translator, *The Essential Haiku: Versions of Basho, Buson, & Issa* (New York, NY, Ecco, 1995)

Higginson, William J. and Harter, Penny, *The Haiku Handbook: How to Write, Teach, and Appreciate Haiku* (Tokyo, Kodansha, 1985) (A classic!)

Kacian, Jim, et al., editors, *Haiku in English—The First Hundred Years* (New York, NY, W. W. Norton & Co., 2013)

Kacian, Jim, *How to Haiku*, (Winchester, VA, Red Moon Press, 2006). Published online: thehaikufoundation.org/omeka/items/show/164

Lanoue, David G., *Write Haiku Like Issa: A Haiku How-To* (New Orleans, LA, David G. Lanoue, 2017)

Mason, Scott, *The Wonder Code: Discover the Way of Haiku and See the World with New Eyes* (Chappaqua, NY, Girasole Press, 2017)

Reichhold, Jane, *Writing and Enjoying Haiku, A Hands-on Guide* (New York, NY, Kodansha, 2013) (Note: This book is my favorite, especially for beginners. It has an interesting section on using various techniques to help write effective haiku.)

Root-Bernstein, Michele, and Banwarth, Francine, *The Haiku Life* (Lincoln, IL, Modern Haiku Press, 2017)

Ross, Bruce, editor, *Haiku Moment: An Anthology of Contemporary North American Haiku* (Rutland, VT, Charles E. Tuttle Co. Inc., 1993)

Ross, Bruce, *Writing Haiku: A Beginner's Guide to Composing Japanese Poetry* (North Clarendon, VT, Tuttle, 2022)

Van den Heuvel, Cor, editor, *The Haiku Anthology* (New York, NY, W. W. Norton & Co., 1999)

Wakan, Naomi Beth, *The Way of Haiku* (Brunswick, ME, Shanti Arts Publishing, 2019)

Welch, Michael Dylan, *Becoming a Haiku Poet* (Sammamish, WA, Michael Dylan Welch, 2015)

Bibliography
Recommended Haiku Books
for Younger Children

Donegan, Patricia, *Write Your Own Haiku* (Rutland, VT, Tuttle, 2005, 2017). With almost identical content, also published as: *Haiku—Asian Arts & Crafts for Creative Kids* (Rutland, VT, Tuttle, 2003)

Manley, Curtis, *Climbing the Volcano: A Journey in Haiku* (New York, NY, Neal Porter Books/Holiday House, 2024); illustrations by Jennifer K. Mann

Ramirez-Christensen, Esperanza, translator, *My First Book of Haiku Poems* (Rutland, VT, Tuttle, 2019); a picture book of 20 classic poems by Japanese haiku masters; illustrations by Tracy Gallup

Rosenberg, Sydell, *H is for Haiku: A Treasury of Haiku from A to Z* (Oklahoma City, OK, Penny Candy Books, 2018); illustrations by Sawsan Chalabi

Further Exploration
Journals, Organizations, Websites, and Presses
(not an exhaustive list)

PRINTED JOURNALS

Acorn: A Journal of Contemporary Haiku
acornhaiku.com

Blithe Spirit: Journal of the British Haiku Society
britishhaikusociety.org.uk/journal

Bottle Rockets
bottlerocketspress.com

First Frost
firstfrostpoetry.com

Frogpond: Journal of the Haiku Society of America
hsa-haiku.org/frogpond

Hedgerow: A Journal of Small Poems
hedgerowhaiku.com

The Heron's Nest
theheronsnest.com/archives.html
(printed annual compilations)

Kingfisher
kingfisherjournal.com

Mayfly
brooksbookshaiku.com/mayfly.html

Modern Haiku
modernhaiku.org

Poetry Pea Journal
poetrypea.com
(journals available as pdf documents)

Presence
haikupresence.org

Seashores
haikuspirit.org/seashores.html

Trash Panda
trashpandahaiku.org

ONLINE JOURNALS

Autumn Moon Haiku Journal
autumnmoonhaiku.com

Cattails
cattailsjournal.com/currentissue.html

Chrysanthemum
chrysanthemum-haiku.net/en

Cold Moon Journal
coldmoonjournal.blogspot.com

Haiku in Action
nickvirgiliohaiku.org/haiku-in-action

The Heron's Nest
theheronsnest.com
(quarterly issues online)

Juxtapositions
thehaikufoundation.org/juxta

The Pan Haiku Review
callofthepage.org/the-pan-haiku-review
(issued in pdf)

Shadow Pond Journal
shadowpondjournal.blogspot.com

Tinywords
Haiku & Other Small Poems
tinywords.com

Tsuri-Doro
A Small Journal of Haiku and Senryu
tsuridoro.org

Under the Basho
underthebasho.com

Wales Haiku Journal
waleshaikujournal.com

There are also journals dedicated to *haiga*, *haibun*, *senryu*,
and *tanka*. In addition, several haiku journals that have
ceased operation have left their archived issues online for
all to read, e.g., *Shamrock Haiku Journal*, *A Hundred Gourds*,
and *Simply Haiku*, among others.

HAIKU ORGANIZATIONS
(not an exhaustive list)

American Haiku Archives
americanhaikuarchives.org

Association Francophone de Haiku
association-francophone-de-haiku.com

Australian Haiku Society
australianhaikusociety.org

British Haiku Society
britishhaikusociety.org.uk

Haiku Canada
haikucanada.org

The Haiku Foundation
thehaikufoundation.org

Haiku North America
haikunorthamerica.com

Haiku Society of America
hsa-haiku.org

New Zealand Poetry Society (Haiku NZ)
poetrysociety.org.nz/haiku-happenings

Triveni Haikai India
trivenihaikai.in

Yuki Teikei Haiku Society
yths.org

HAIKU RESOURCES ONLINE
(a sampling)

The Haiku Foundation
thehaikufoundation.org

The Living Haiku Anthology
livinghaikuanthology.com

The Living Senryu Anthology
senryu.life

AHAPoetry
ahapoetry.com

Graceguts
graceguts.com/haiku-and-senryu

NaHaiWriMo
nahaiwrimo.com/national-haiku-writing-month

HAIKU PRESSES
(a sampling)

Brooks Books
brooksbookshaiku.com

Modern Haiku Press
modernhaiku.org/mhbooks

Red Moon Press
redmoonpress.com

Snapshot Press
snapshotpress.co.uk

Why This Book Came to Be

TO GATHER MY SCATTERED POEMS

Browsing the heaps of haiku collections offered for sale at a recent Haiku North America conference (most books either self-published or published by small haiku presses), I realized how rewarding it must feel for poets to gather a selection of their scattered poems into one book. Haiku poets typically start their publishing journeys with single poems getting printed in several different journals. Short collections are often released in chapbook form or as e-books. Poets sometimes win publication as a prize in a contest sponsored by a haiku press. Half of the haiku in this book were taken from my manuscript "Pond Ripples," which earned an honorable mention in the Sable Books' International Women's Haiku Contest 2021, judged by Kala Ramesh, an esteemed poet skilled in several types of Japanese short-form poetry. The press published the contest's first-place winner.

TO SERVE AS A RESOURCE AND TEXTBOOK

When teaching haiku as a guest speaker in a school, I have about one hour to introduce haiku to students and get them to write haiku, too. I need dozens of appealing haiku for a reading, for discussion, and to use as examples to illustrate the various points I make in the lesson. I want the poems' content to resonate with students in grades three and up. This collection is an excellent resource for that purpose. This is not a collection of haiku-like poems written for children's picture books, as some authors have done. I intend this collection of (mostly) previously published poems to spark imagination, discussion, and a desire to try writing quality haiku—for children *and* adults. I hope you enjoyed them.

About the Author

ANNA EKLUND-CHEONG

Fascinated by haiku since seventh grade, Anna started writing them in earnest in 2015. With over 130 haiku now published in 19 journals, she felt it was time to gather most of them under one cover in her first collection. A graduate of the University of Minnesota, she has worked in public and academic libraries and in customer service and marketing for a law books publisher. Her family of four moved from St. Paul, MN, to Stamford, CT, and then to Croissy-sur-Seine, France, near Versailles. In Paris, she volunteers with several anglophone cultural organizations, teaches haiku classes for adults and children, and leads occasional tours called Benjamin Franklin's Paris. Now grandparents, she and her husband travel frequently to their Maryland home in the US to be with their growing family, when not exploring the ancient sites and cultural monuments of Europe and beyond.

MORE OF HER WORK CAN BE FOUND ONLINE
The Living Haiku Anthology
The Living Senryu Anthology
Haiku Registry of The Haiku Foundation

WEBSITE parishaiku.com
INSTAGRAM @parishaiku
EMAIL parishaiku@gmail.com